THE ORGANS AND ORGANISTS OF ST MARY'S CHURCH BURY ST EDMUNDS, SUFFOLK

Peter Tryon

With memories of St Mary's Choir written by former choristers

Honey Hill Publishing
St Mary's Church, Honey Hill, Bury St Edmunds, Suffolk IP33 1RT, UK.

First published in 2001 by Honey Hill Publishing.

This revised edition published in 2008 by Honey Hill Publishing.

Acknowledgements

A large amount of material contained in this booklet has come originally from the 1960s publication by Norman Jones entitled 'A Short History of the Organ'. A huge debt of gratitude is expressed for his pioneering work.

The author also wishes to acknowledge the help given by David Weston on the organists of St Mary's, and the technical information from Mr Kenneth Canter.

This publication has been sponsored by St Mary's Heritage Committee who, together with Honey Hill Publishing, would like to thank Amanda Scott for her enthusiastic assistance with its production.

Photographs on the front cover and pages 10,15 and 17 are by
Ricky Wilkinson, MBE.

ISBN 978 0 9554504 0 2

Honey Hill Publishing is an enterprise of St Mary's Church, Bury St Edmunds, Suffolk, UK.

Foreword

At the present time the pipe organ is under considerable pressure to survive, let alone flourish, at any rate within the context of English parish churches. The cost of regular tuning, maintenance and renewal can be considerable, and a burden upon a congregation. Facing the prospect of a major rebuild is enough to strike terror into the hearts of any PCC, and at that stage the inevitable solution may well be the abandonment of the instrument.

A second factor which has led to the decline of the pipe organ is the perception — influenced by the desire to modernize everything as we enter the new century — that it is old-fashioned and fuddy-duddy. Furthermore, during the last three decades or so there has been an increasing movement away from 'traditional' Anglican church music in favour of hymns and songs which, it is thought, are more generally acceptable in today's culture, especially amongst younger people. Many of these newer compositions are simply not suitable for pipe organ accompaniment.

Considerations of this sort have persuaded many churches to opt for other forms of musical instrument for worship. The electronic organ represents a comparatively modest outlay for a PCC. Much less expensive, and much more flexible in accompanying modern songs, is the music group, which may vary from a flute and two or three recorders, to a battery of electric guitars, keyboard, drums, and who knows what, according to resources available.

Actually, there is nothing new in the idea of a music group, since bands were fairly common in parish churches during the late 1700s and early 1800s. As Peter Tryon remarks, there may even have been one in St Mary's at that time!

This being no place for discussing the merits of various instruments, we are content to record our satisfaction and gratitude that, thanks to the efforts, expertise and generosity of many people over the years, we have in

St Mary's a very fine pipe organ which, it is to be hoped, we shall continue to maintain and utilize to the full.

A fine organ is of little value without a competent organist to exploit its qualities, and a shortage of such people is another reason why some churches have put aside their organs. As the roll of honour in this booklet makes clear, St Mary's has enjoyed a succession of talented exponents of the keyboards.

Finally, our church would be immeasurably poorer without its choir to lead the worship. So we give thanks for an extraordinary choral history of several hundred years, and for the long line of individuals who have served within it, some of them for many years. The contributions which we are publishing are necessarily limited in number, but well illustrate a strong sense of devotion and duty to God and to his church — not to mention an abundance of personal satisfaction and enjoyment.

Lance Bidewell
St Mary's Heritage Committee

The Organs of St Mary's Church

'In the beginning ...'

References in wills, to priests singing for the repose of souls at St Mary's, occur as early as 1354, after which there are many references to singers and 'chylds with a surplys'.

The first primary evidence for an organ in St Mary's is in the will of John Baret, who died in 1467. (Baret's macabre memorial can be seen in the south aisle.) He willed that 'eche man yt synggit prykked[1] songe of ye daye of my enterment at oure ladyes messe haue ij d. and ye pleyers at ye orgenys ij d.'[2] This plurality may refer to there having been two organs in the church, or even to the fact that there was one organ with double bellows. Organs in those days were always referred to as 'a pair', rather like a pair of scissors. In 1479 Thomas Cranewys bequeathed the organist 10d.

Tymms, in his 1845 guide to the church, suggests that there were two organs, situated over the epistle and gospel doorways, but there is no concrete evidence to support this. It was, however, not an unusual arrangement, as we know that Long Melford had two organs on the rood screen for accompanying chanted parts of the services.

There is no description of the instrument(s), the first specification of an organ in Britain not occurring until 1519.[3] However, we can be fairly certain that it (they) only had one manual of limited compass and was probably a small portative[4] instrument of no more than three stops. During the Commonwealth period (1649-60) most organs were destroyed by the Puritans. St Mary's organ must have gone the same way, although

---

1 This was part music, not plainchant.

2 Dinner was also provided!

3 All Hallows, Barking – 3 stops – diapason Xft, double principal Vft.

4 Portable – usually on a table.

Tuning a Portative

we believe that there was still a choir of sorts for the annual Jankyn Smyth service.

No other references in parish records to an organ occur until 1802, although there are records of singing boys and a master to teach them. St James' did have an organ in 1760 and it is seems unlikely that St Mary's would not have had one also. Perhaps, however, there was no organ and the church had a band to accompany the services? They were certainly popular at the time. In 1777, at the beating of the parish boundaries, 14 gallons of beer was consumed by the men and boys of the choir!

In 1802 Ralph Guest, the boy's singing master, was instructed to 'procure an organ to accompany the singing boys in the psalms at a price not exceeding 100 guineas'. This was a fairly sizeable sum in those days and would have provided a one- or two-manual organ of around ten to twelve stops. A Bury guide of 1821 stated that the church contained a small organ. No details exist of the instrument, although the back can just be seen in a contemporary painting which hangs in the tower meeting room. It was obviously fairly transportable, since it was tried out in various positions on the galleries which stood over the north and south aisles, finally resting above the tower doorway. Its final fate is unknown, although there are some old 18th-century stops in the choir organ of the present instrument (nazard, tierce) [5] which may belong to that instrument, but this seems unlikely.

The Gray Organ

---

[5] Records state that the organ was sold for £150, but do not say where it went. Unsubstantiated suggestions as to its whereabouts have included the organ being placed in the then chapel of ease in St Mary's Square or incorporated in the organ of Garland Street Baptist Chapel.

In 1825 a west gallery was constructed which occupied the third bay from the back of the nave. A new organ was installed in 1826 from public subscription at a cost of around £1,000.[6] In an inventory of 1828 it is referred to as 'large finger[7] organ by Gray with brass rods, pillars, crimson curtains and organ stool'. No specification exists, although we can identify five stops on the present great organ. The Gray organ probably consisted of two manuals.

The choice of John Gray of London to build the new organ was an inspired one. Gray was one of the foremost organ builders of his day, and this indicates that St Mary's wanted the very best available. It is probable that the organ came by water from London and was landed at Ipswich, travelling the rest of the way by horse and cart. In 1838 the firm became known as Gray and Davidson.

In September 1826 Mr Nunn, the organist of the church, organized a series of concerts to celebrate the installation of the organ, with sacred music in the morning at the church and secular concerts in the evening at the Theatre Royal. These concerts were very well attended, with an average of 1,800 people at St Mary's and 700 at the Theatre Royal, and they raised a substantial sum of money for the recently completed West Suffolk Hospital. Two years later he attempted to repeat the concerts with £3,000 guaranteed by himself and friends, but they were only about one-third full and became a financial embarrassment. Probably the reason was that the concerts were held during the October Fair and tickets were priced at half a guinea, far more than the previous time.

An interesting newspaper article of the time speaks in glowing terms of the quality of the opening concert on 19 September 1826. There are also some clues in this about the organ: 'We scarcely ever remember to have heard an organ where the three great requisites — grandeur, brilliancy and smoothness — were so successfully combined. The majesty and fullness of the great diapasons, the brilliance and rapid articulation of the full organ, and the smoothness of the fancy stops, are equally striking.

---

[6] The organ cost £826. The gallery must have cost £174.

[7] No pedals or barrel mechanism.

Amongst the latter we cannot help praising the cremona,[8] for the uniform sweetness of its tone'... It must certainly have sounded very fine in such a commanding position.

During the church restoration of 1843-4, the west gallery was demolished and the organ was re-erected on a gallery on the north side, three bays from the west end (an identical position to the former organ). The move incorporated various improvements and these included the reconstruction of the key movement so as to place the organist several feet in advance of his instrument. The organ was in the care of Gray and Davidson, who made sundry additions over the following years.

By 1864, when T.B.Richardson was appointed organist, it must have been in a terrible state, for it drew forth this comment from J.S. Hopkins of Trinity College, Cambridge who had adjudicated in the matter of the appointment: 'I ought in justice to Mr Richardson, draw attention to the very unsatisfactory state of the organ, which, in addition to being totally deficient of all the improvements so much needed for the playing of pure organ music, is in parts much dilapidated and in such dirty condition that the tone (which appears to be generally good) is much lessened both in quality and quantity from what it ought to be.' This roused the church authorities into immediate action.

The Walker Rebuilds

In 1865, an estimate by J.W.Walker of London for £560 was accepted for the enlargement of the organ and the addition of a piccolo stop. The piccolo stop was a gift of Mr Richardson and still exists in the choir organ. At the same time, the organ appears to have been moved to its present position, but at ground level. The central part of the Gray case was incorporated into the design and can now be seen above the gates to the Regimental Chapel (it was originally placed on the east side of the chapel). A large spotted metal diapason was installed on the great organ to provide a pipe rack in the chancel. It was a major rebuild, almost certainly adding the third manual and pedals. We have it from Walker's records that

---

[8] A cremona sounds like a clarinet.

nearly all the old pipework was retained. The action was tracker to the manuals and pneumatic to the pedals.

Specification of the Organ in 1865

Great Organ

1. Double Diapason	16
2. Open Diapason (large)	8
3. Open Diapason (small)*	8
4. Gamba	8
5. Stopped Diapason	8
6. Principal *	4
7. Flute	4
8. Twelfth *	2⅔
9. Fifteenth*	2
10. Full Mixture*	IV
11. Sharp Mixture	II
12. Trumpet	8
13. Clarion	4

Coupler: Swell to Great

Swell Organ

14. Sub Bass	16
15. Open Diapason	8
16. Keraulophon	8
17. Stopped Diapason	8
18. Principal	4
19. Celestina	4
20. Gamba	2
21. Mixture	III
22. Oboe	8
23. Horn	8
24. Clarion	4

Choir Organ

25. Open Diapason	8
26. Lieblich Gedeckt	8
27. Dulciana	8
28. Viola Da Gamba	8
29. Principal	4
30. Flute	4
31. Piccolo	2
32. Cremona (TC)	8

Pedal Organ

33. Open Diapason	16
34. Bourdon	16
35. Violone	8
36. Trombone	16

Couplers: Great to Pedal
Swell to Pedal
Choir to Pedal

* Definitely by Gray

In 1880 three stops were added: Swell Organ, vox humana 8; Choir Organ, vox angelica 8; Pedal Organ, violone 16. A thin-toned tuba was also added to the choir organ some time later. In 1885 sums were paid to Walker for 'repairs and additions', and then a fairly major rebuild took place in 1898. The organ now had 41 speaking stops, 6 couplers and a tremulant. The action was still tracker, but the bottom 1½ octaves on the great organ, tuba, as well as the pedals, were pneumatic. 3½-inch wind pressure was used to the manuals, and 6½-inch wind pressure to the pedal stops, tuba and pneumatics. The organ was opened by G.W.M. Boutell, organist of the church, and remained in the hands of J.W. Walker until 1931. By all accounts the tone of the organ, particularly the great diapasons, was very fine, except that the great organ mixture work was considered to be rather shrill.

The Hill, Norman and Beard Rebuild

By 1931 there was a need to increase the volume of sound to cope with the increasing demands of large civic services. Fortunately £4,000 was made available through the generosity of the late Robert Plumpton, who owned an ironmonger's in the town, Andrews and Plumpton. £1,000 was earmarked to be invested for the future upkeep of the organ.

A number of schemes were considered, the most ambitious being by Willis, who proposed dividing the organ either side of the chancel on raised platforms. Unfortunately the money was not sufficient to have allowed this to take place. Another serious contender was Nicholsons of Worcester, who proposed a comprehensive three-manual scheme, including a 32ft sub-bass, for £2,700 (details in the Record Office). However, a final decision was made to award the scheme to Hill, Norman and Beard for £3,200. At the same time the opportunity was taken to raise the organ on a platform and so provide access to the Suffolk Regimental Chapel. The chapel was decorated by Sir Ninian Comper, who also designed some cases for the organ but, unfortunately, these have never been provided. The designs may be seen on the wall of St Mary's song school.

The rebuild was a colossal affair. The entire internal layout, frame and solo organ were new. The action was tubular pneumatic throughout, and adjustable thumb pistons were provided. The four-manual console retained its original position behind the choirstalls. Also provided was a 7½-hp duplex blower, housed in a chamber outside the church. This motor is still operating.

Specification of the Organ in 1933

Great Organ

1. Violone	16
2. Open Diapason I	8
3. Open Diapason II	8
4. Open Diapason III	8
5. Claribel Flute	8
6. Corno Flute	8
7. Principal	4
8. Harmonic Flute	4
9. Twelfth	$2^{2}/_{3}$
10. Fifteenth	2
11. Mixture	IV
12. Tromba	8
13. Tuba (Solo)	8
14. Clarion	4

Couplers: Swell to Great
Swell Octave to Great
Swell Sub Octave to Great
Solo to Great
Solo Octave to Great
Solo Sub Octave to Great
Choir to Great
Choir Octave to Great
Choir Sub Octave to Great

Swell Organ

15. Bourdon	16
16. Open Diapason	8
17. Rohr Flute	8
18. Echo Gamba	8
19. Voix Celeste (TC)	8
20. Principal	4
21. Harmonic Gedeckt	4
22. Super Octave	2
23. Fifteenth (new 1959)	2
24. Mixture	III
25. Oboe	8
Tremulant	
26. Double Trumpet	16
27. Harmonic Horn	8
28. Trumpet (ext 25)	8
29. Octave Trumpet (ext 27)	4

Couplers: Octave
Sub Octave
Solo to Swell
Solo Octave to Swell
Solo Sub Octave to Swell

Choir Organ (enclosed)

30. Contra Dulciana	16
31. Open Diapason	8
32. Dulciana (ext 30)	8
33. Leiblich Gedeckt	8
34. Viola da Gamba	8
35. Unda Maris (TC)	8
36. Octave Geigen	4
37. Dulcet (ext 32)	4
38. Hohl Flute	4
39. Nazard	$2^{2}/_{3}$
40. Septième (ext 37)	$2^{2}/_{7}$
41. Piccolo	2
42. Tierce	$1^{3}/_{5}$
Tremulant	
43. Tromba (Great)	8
44. Clarion (Great)	4

Couplers: Octave
Sub Octave
Swell to Choir
Swell Octave to Choir
Swell Sub Octave to Choir
Solo to Choir
Solo Octave to Choir
Solo Sub Octave to Choir

Solo Organ (enclosed)

45. Harmonic Claribel	8
46. Viol d'Orchestre	8
47. String Celeste (TG)	8
48. Concert Flute	4
49. Orchestral Oboe	8
50. Clarinett	8
Tremulant	
51. Tuba	8

Couplers: Octave
Sub Octave

Pedal Organ

52. Acoustic Bass (out 1959)	32
53. Open Diapason (metal)	16
54. Open Diapason (wood)	16
55. Violone (Great)	16
56. Bourdon	
57. Echo Bourdon	16
58. Dulciana (Choir)	16
59. Octave (Ext 53)	8
60. Bass Flute	8
61. Dulciana (Choir)	8
62. Flute Octaviante	4
63. Double Trumpet (Swell)	16
64. Trombone	16
65. Tuba (Solo)	8

Couplers: Great to Pedal
Swell to Pedal
Swell Octave to Pedal
Choir to Pedal
Choir Octave to Pedal
Solo to Pedal

However, by 1957 there were signs that all was not well with the action as sundry notes remained silent. On investigation it was found that the pneumatic work had been affected by sulphur fumes and damp. In 1959 the John Compton Organ company cleaned the organ, added electric action to the pneumatics and provided a detached console, retaining much of the original fittings in its design. The only tonal changes were a fifteenth on the swell to replace the vox humana and the removal of the acoustic bass. The original console space was fitted out as a choir library.

A General View of the Organ

There were considerable advantages in the console now being detached, but its movement was limited to a few feet by an extremely thick cable.

By all accounts the organ never really worked satisfactorily after 1959, as the original pneumatic leatherwork had been retained and continued to be patched and repatched. Problems with the electrics also meant that cyphers[9] occurred, and odd notes would slip in unannounced! The sound was also stifled because of the position of the pedal organ facing directly into the nave, making the organ bottom-heavy. In fact, the pedal trombone was so loud (despite toning down from Comptons), that it obliterated everything else.

---

[9] Notes sticking on.

Tonal changes were made by John Norman for Hill, Norman and Beard in the early 1970s when the great flutes were replaced by a new stopped diapason 8ft and chimney flute 4ft. These were typical of the baroque revival of the period and 'chiffed'[10] far too much. They were toned down at the later rebuild to match the rest of the organ. Another tonal change was a II-rank-sharp mixture on the swell instead of the fifteenth. This was never in tune and did not balance with the rest of the organ. By the 1980s matters were becoming serious and a number of failures occurred.

The Canter Rebuild

After careful consideration of a number of options, the contract to rebuild the organ was awarded to Kenneth Canter of Thurston. Kenncth had originally been trained with Walkers and had been their Midlands manager before setting up his own business some twenty years previously. He was assisted in his work by Michael Harrison (another ex-Walker employee), David Broom, (voicer) and Jeffrey Heard (electronics). It was a decision we have never regretted for one moment. The work was carried out with meticulous care and professionalism, at a cost of around £50,000.

The priority of the 1988 rebuild was to make the organ reliable. For this reason the Compton electrics were completely replaced and every single secondary pneumatic was disposed of. The whole organ could now operate with an efficient and reliable electro-pneumatic action controlled through a Christie transmission system computer. This also meant that the console could be fully mobile, with only a simple co-axil lead connection. At the same time, the piston system was upgraded with 64 channels of memory. The confusing array of intermanual couplers was discarded, the octave couplers now acting straight through the ordinary couplers (like a mechanical action organ).

The organ was thoroughly cleaned and regulated, and small tonal changes were made to bring it more up to date with current thinking. The tone of the organ was carefully preserved, making this primarily a 1930s romantic organ whose main task was the accompaniment of worship.

---

[10] Spoke with an initial pop!

Specification of the organ in 1988

Great Organ

Stop		Rank
1. Violone	16	A
2. Open Diapason I	8	
3. Open Diapason II	8	
4. Open Diapason III	8	
5. Open Diapason IV	8	A*
6. Stopped Diapason	8	
7. Octave	4	
8. Principal	4	A*
9. Chimney Flute	4	
10. Twelfth	$2\frac{2}{3}$	
11. Fifteenth	2	
12. Seventeenth	$1\frac{3}{5}$	*
13. Mixture 19,22,26,29	IV	
14. Bombarde	8	
15. Posaune	4	

Couplers: Swell to Great
Choir to Great
Solo to Great

Swell Organ

Stop		Rank
16. Bourdon	16	
17. Open Diapason	8	
18. Rohr Flute	8	
19. Echo Gamba	8	
20. Voix Celeste (TC)	8	
21. Principal	4	
22. Harmonic Gedeckt	4	
23. Super Octave	2	
24. Larigot	$1\frac{1}{3}$	*
25. Mixture 15,19,22	III	
26. Oboe	8	
Tremulant		
27. Double Trumpet	16	B
28. Harmonic Horn	8	
29. Trumpet	8	B
30. Octave Trumpet	4	B

Couplers: Octave
Sub Octave
Unison off
Solo to Swell

Choir Organ (enclosed)

Stop		Rank
31. Contra Dulciana	16	C
32. Open Diapason	8	
33. Dulciana	8	C
34. Lieblich Gedeckt	8	
35. Viola da Gamba	8	
36. Flute Celeste (TC)	8	*
37. Octave Geigen	4	
38. Dulcet	4	C
39. Hohl Flute	4	
40. Nazard	$2\frac{2}{3}$	
41. Dulcetina	2	C*
42. Piccolo	2	
43. Tierce	$1\frac{3}{5}$	
44. Octavin	1	C*
Tremulant		
45. Tuba Magna (Solo)	8	
46. Bombarde (Great)	8	
47. Posaune (Great)	4	

Couplers: Octave
Sub Octave
Unison off
Swell to Choir
Solo to Choir

Solo Organ (enclosed)

	Rank
48. Harmonic Claribel	8
49. Viol d'Orchestre	8
50. String Celeste (TG)	8
51. Concert Flute	4
52. Orchestral Oboe	8
53. Clarinet	8
Tremulant	
54. Tuba	8

Couplers: Octave
Sub Octave
Unison off

Pedal Organ

55. Open Metal	16	D
56. Open Wood	16	E
57. Violone	16	A
58. Bourdon	16	
59. Echo Bourdon	16	
60. Dulciana	16	C
61. Quint	$10^2/_3$	*
62. Principal	8	D*
63. Violone	8	A*
64. Octave	8	E
65. Bass Flute	8	
66. Dulciana	8	C
67. Fifteenth	4	D*
68. Viola	4	A*
69. Flute Octaviante	4	
70. Furniture 19,22,26,29	IV	*
71. Contra Trombone	32	F*
72. Trombone	16	F*
73. Double Trumpet	16	B
74. Tuba (Solo)	8	
75. Cornett	4	B*

Couplers: Great to Pedal
Swell to Pedal
Choir to Pedal
Solo to Pedal

Accessories:
7 thumb and toe pistons to Grt and Ped
7 thumb and toe pistons to Swell
7 thumb pistons to Choir
7 general thumb pistons
5 thumb pistons to Solo
1 general cancel thumb piston
Reversible pistons to all main couplers
Christie 64 channel piston selector
Great and Pedal pistons coupled
Swell and Pedal pistons coupled

Reed Pressures:
Great 7½ inch
Swell 8 inch
Solo Tuba 16½ inch
Pedal Trombone 8½ inch

Flue Pressures:
Great 4 inch
Swell 3½ inch
Choir $3^3/_4$ inch
Solo 6 inch
Pedal 4 inch

Compass:
Manuals: CC-C 61 notes
Pedals: CCC-F 30 notes

*New in 1988

Tonal changes included:

Great Organ: flutes revoiced, open IV and second principal added; corno flute transposed as a $1^3/_5$ seventeenth; mixture toned down; reeds renamed; tuba transferred to choir organ.

Swell Organ: sharp mixture out, larigot $1^1/_3$ in; horn rebuilt.

Choir Organ: dulciana extended to include a dulcetina 2ft and an octavin 1ft; septième removed, having no useful purpose; unda maris replaced with a second-hand flute celeste 8ft from Ashby-de-la- Zouch Parish Church.

Solo Organ: tuba renamed tuba magna 8ft.

Pedal Organ: echo bourdon transposed to a true quint $10^2/_3$; open diapasons renamed; open metal extended to 8ft and 4ft pitches; violone made available at 8ft and 4ft pitches; new IV-rank furniture installed where the trombone stood; new metal trombone 16ft provided, but placed on the choir box, and old trombone remade as a 32ft extension (half length).

The instrument was duly opened in September 1988 with a recital by Martin Neary, Organist and Master of the Choristers at Westminster Abbey. Since then, it has proved itself extremely reliable, despite heavy use since the rebuild, and a continual delight to all who have the pleasure to play it.

However, there are plans to have further work done in the near future. This is likely to include a thorough cleaning, the replacement of the Christie Transmission System with a new, more reliable and faster system, a new blower and associated electrics, some releathering of the stop and under actions, new vertical shutters on the swell box, and possibly a new nave section behind the Gray casework to send sound into the nave to support large congregations. These changes will also hopefully include bringing the Tuba out of the solo box and remaking the pedal 32ft reed. It is also hoped to tidy up the casework.

Addendum to *The Organs and Organists of St Mary's Church, Bury St Edmunds*

In 2009, the Christie Transmission System failed and was replaced with a new 250 channel musicom system. This allowed for certain extras such as a stepper, some new stops, swell on swell and a transposer. The work was carried out by Warren Marsh of Clevedon Organ Services.
With the installation of a new organ at the cathedral, the old Nicholson Trompetta Real ** was purchased and will be installed when funds allow.
The current specification is as follows:

The Organ in St Mary's Church, Bury St Edmunds, Suffolk, UK

Great Organ

No.	Stop	Pitch
1	Contra Violone TC	32*
2	Violone	16C
3	Open Diapason no.1	8
4	Open Diapason no.2	8
5	Open Diapason no.3	8
6	Open Diapason no.4	8C
7	Stopped Diapason	8
8	Quint	5.1/3 *
9	Octave	4
10	Principal	4C
11	Chimney Flute	4
12	Twelfth	2.2/3
13	Fifteenth	2
14	Seventeenth	1.3/5
15	Mixture 19,22,26,29	IV
16	Ophicleide	16*
17	Bombarde	8
18	Posaune	4

Grt Octave Sw-Grt. Ch-Grt So-Grt

Choir Organ (enclosed)

No.	Stop	Pitch
35	Contra Dulciana	16D
36	Open Diapason	8
37	Lieblich Gedeckt	8
38	Viola da Gamba	8
39	Dulciana	8D
40	Flute Celeste TC	8
41	Geigen Principal	4
42	Hohl Flue	4
43	Dulcet	4D

Swell Organ

No.	Stop	Pitch
19	Bourdon	16
20	Open Diapason	8
21	Rohr Flute	8
22	Echo Gamba	8
23	Voix Celeste TC	8
24	Principal	4
25	Lieblich Flute	4
26	Super Octave	2
27	Octavin	1*
28	Mixture 15,19,22	III
29	Oboe	8
30	Tremulant	
31	Double Trumpet	16F
32	Harmonic Horn	8
33	Trumpet	8F
34	Octave Trumpet	4F

So-Sw Oct Sub Unison off

Solo Organ (enclosed)

No.	Stop	Pitch
53	Harmonic Claribel	8
54	Viol D'Orchestre	8
55	Viole Celeste GG	8
56	Concert Flute	4
57	Orchestral Oboe	8
58	Clarinet	8
59	Tremulant	
60	Harmonic Horn (Sw)	8*
61	Tuba Magna (16" WGP)	8
62	Trompetta Real (Unenclosed)	8**

Oct Sub Unison off

44	Nazard	2.2/3
45	Piccolo	2
46	Dulcetina	2 D
47	Tierce	1.3/5
48	Larigot	1.1/3 *
49	Tremulant	
50	Bombarde (Great)	8
51	Posaune (Great)	4
52	Tuba Magna (Solo)	8

So-Ch Sw-Ch Oct Sub Unison off

Electro Pneumatic Action
Full compliment of pistons
Detached Console
250 channel memory
Compass: 61/30
Stepper
Swell on Swell
Transposer
All pistons next

*New 2009

Pedal Organ

63	Contra Bass	32*
64	Open Metal	16A
65	Open Wood	16B
66	Violone	16C
67	Bourdon	16
68	Dulciana	16D
69	Quint	10.2/3
70	Principal	8A
71	Octave	8B
72	Violone	8C
73	Bass Flute	8
74	Dulciana	8D
75	Fifteenth	4A
76	Viola	4C
77	Flute Octaviante	4
78	Furniture 19,22,26,29	IV
79	Contra Trombone	32E
80	Trombone	16E
81	Double Trumpet	16F
82	Tuba (Solo)	8
83	Cornett (Sw Horn)	4*

Grt-Ped Sw-Ped Ch-Ped So-Ped

The wide variety of sounds the organ produces is a fine testament to the excellence of workmanship which this and former generations have lavished upon it. It is currently in the care of Warren Marsh of Brandon.

The Organ Console

The Chamber Organ

In 1995 the opportunity arose to purchase a chamber organ for the Lady Chapel. A small instrument was needed when only a few people attended a service and music was required, and the Lady Chapel offered a much more intimate atmosphere. The organ could also be used for concerts as a continuo instrument.

The organ was purchased for £400 from the vicar of St Michael, Camden Town, London. He had seen it (in bits) being used as part of the Christmas decorations at a chapel in Neasden. Reconstructing it in the church, he replaced the missing pipes from a Compton organ in a redundant church being used by a Greek Orthodox congregation, also in Camden.

Under the direction of Kenneth Canter, the organ was moved from London on a choir parent's lorry and placed on a moveable base, which was kindly donated by a Stanton firm. A blower was provided which originally came from the Railway Mission on the Fornham Road. Apart from new tuning slides, the instrument has received little attention. Hopefully a full restoration will be undertaken soon, when its history can be properly researched.

The casework is probably dated around 1800 and has almost certainly come from a variety of different instruments. However, the instrument is considerably older and may be the work of John Harris (c.1677-1743), son of the famous organ builder Renatus. John's most famous organs were at St Mary Redcliffe, Bristol and Doncaster Parish Church. If this organ is by Harris, it is one of the oldest organs in the country and a national treasure.

The compass of the organ is 56 notes (CC-G) but was certainly longer by at least three notes in the bass (short compass BAG). The keyboard is not original. The action is mechanical.

The specification is:

Open Diapason 8ft (Middle C upwards)
Stopped Diapason 8ft
Principal 4ft
Fifteenth 2ft

The Chamber Organ

The Organists of St Mary's

Ralph Guest 1796–1822

Ralph Guest was born in 1742 at Broseley, Shropshire, where he later became a chorister in the parish church. Upon attaining his majority he left for London, where he was engaged in commercial pursuits. At the same time he joined the choir of Portland Chapel.

At the age of 26 he came to Bury to set up his own business, obtaining organ lessons at the same time from Mr Ford, organist of St James. He devoted himself entirely to music when he was appointed in 1796 as Master of the Singing Boys, and was instructed to procure an organ in 1802 to accompany the singing boys in the psalms. He published *The Psalms of David*, arranged for every day of the month. This used many old tunes and sixty new ones composed by himself. According to parish records he was a bit of a 'Jack of all trades', being employed to make alterations to the choir stalls, alter the pews in the gallery, and do other jobs in the church.

Guest died in June 1830 at the advanced age of 88. His son George (1771-1831) became a chorister of the Chapel Royal, and subsequently organist of Eye Parish Church in 1787 and Wisbech in 1789. No doubt he knew Robert Nunn.

Robert Nunn 1822–1863

Robert Nunn was a highly colourful character in the life of Bury St Edmunds and has been likened to Mr Pickwick. In fact he was a great admirer of this Dickens' character, reading each instalment aloud to his family as it was published. How he and his family must have laughed at Mr Pickwick being soaked to the skin outside a girls' boarding school in Westgate Street and his subsequent laying up at the Angel Hotel for rheumatism. Certainly our Mr Nunn, known as 'Old Bob', was an extremely likeable person as well as being highly regarded throughout East Anglia as a musician. He was also somewhat of a practical joker and leg-puller.

Nunn was born at Eye and lived in Bury St Edmunds at a house called St Margaret's, near to Shire Hall (now the home of the Youth Justice Office). In 1823 he had built a large music room, complete with an organ and stage big enough for an orchestra. The room could hold 300 people and concerts were held regularly, with tickets costing seven shillings (twice the price of the best seats in the Theatre Royal). Here was founded the Bury Musical Society.

His son, Robert Lindley Nunn (1826-99), organist of St Mary-le-Tower, Ipswich, wrote of his father: 'In Robert's early days at St Mary's the choir was a dozen boys, whose object, it seemed to me, was to sing as little as possible and crack nuts as often as possible'. Apparently the boys used to collect walnuts on the way to church and throw the shells at the congregation from the gallery! However, within a few years the choir was held in high regard. Mr Nunn's salary in 1827 was £31-10s a year, and was still the same when he died in 1863.

A. Lease 1863–1864

An assistant organist who covered until Thomas Richardson was appointed.

Thomas Bentick Richardson 1864–1893

Richardson, who came from Preston in Lancashire, was appointed after an audition adjudicated by J.S. Hopkins of Trinity College, Cambridge. Twenty-nine people applied for the post, and Richardson was selected from a shortlist of three. In his report to the selection committee, Hopkins stated that he was an effective and good player. His salary was still £31-10s a year in 1877, the organ blower receiving £10 p.a. and the choir expenses totalling £60. By 1890 his salary had steadily risen to £63-7s-11d, but the blower still received £10! During his time, the organ was rebuilt by Walker and moved to its present position.

A memorial brass tablet in the Lady Chapel records his death on 13 April 1893, aged 61 years, having been organist for 29 years.

Mr Kingston 1893(?)–1896

The appointment of Thomas Richardson's successor came swiftly after his death, the post being offered to Mr Owen Clarke of 13 Abbeygate Street on 9 May for £40 p.a. However, by 12 May he had declined the offer for private reasons. Church records now become confused, as the next mention of an organist in the minute book is April 1896 when a Mr Kingston, Mus.Bac. was appointed.

In January 1897 the parish magazine records Mr Kingston's departure to a more remunerative post at Acton Parish Church, stating that he had been organist for 'some time'. This obviously contradicts the statement in the minute book.

Mr George Whitehead was appointed as Kingston's successor. He was an ex-pupil of Richardson and came from Swindon and Marlborough. His arrival was due later in the year, but he only turned up on one or two occasions in June and George Boutell was hurriedly appointed.

George W. Boutell 1897–1909

Boutell arrived in September 1897 from Coventry, where he had been organist and choirmaster at St Mark's Church and sub-organist at St Michael's. (St Michael's was made the cathedral in 1918 and bombed in 1940.)

George Boutell's academic achievements are recorded as FRCO, ARCM. His picture can be seen in the first-ever photograph of the choir taken on 6 July 1903, in which he appears as a flamboyant figure, with a large waxed moustache. Apparently the choir was successful under his command, since there are 26 boys and a staggering 23 men, with the boys all wearing Eton collars.

During this time the choirboys from St Mary's and St Peter's were taken on an annual outing to Great Yarmouth, a special carriage being arranged for them on the train. Dinner and tea would be provided at the Savoy Hotel and each boy was given six pence pocket money.

Boutell's departure in 1909 seems to have been very sudden. There appears to be nothing in the parish magazine about his leaving.

One story that has survived is about his recitals, which were well attended. A favourite piece was Lemmen's 'The Storm'. Apparently he used to produce loud crashing sounds from the organ whilst the verger, Tom Reeve, turned the gas lamps up and down from the mains tap to create the lightning. A rather precarious special effect!

E. Percy Hallam 1909–1937

Born in Nottingham, Percy made a career as an organist after rheumatic fever forced him to give up his intention of being a concert pianist. He played his first service aged 12 and was giving weekly recitals in the Albert Hall, Nottingham at the age of 15. He was a pupil at Manchester Cathedral and took his Mus.Bac. at Durham when aged 19. At 20 he was an FRCO. Prior to coming to Bury he was organist from 1907 to1909 at St Chad's Church, Ladysmith, Manchester. He was appointed to St Mary's in September 1909, aged 21, combining the post with music master at King Edward VI Grammar School. He must have made a very good impression to have been appointed to the post so young, since there had been 100 applicants, with initial interviews held as far afield as London, Sheffield and Yeovil.

Percy was an energetic man, with recreations listed as walking and book collecting. He was also quite highly regarded as a composer, his Magnificat and Nunc Dimittis in A flat being his most famous work, whilst his little anthem 'Thou wilt keep him' is still sung regularly at St Mary's. Everyone who knew Percy speaks highly of him, particularly his ex-pupils at the grammar school. He was affectionately known as 'Porky' Hallam even though he was quite lean. An often repeated story is how he used to throw his hat on the stool and then promptly sit on it, although no one is ever sure whether this was deliberate or not!

In 1937 he was appointed organist at the Cathedral. It was not a post he applied for, and apparently he was virtually told to exchange his loyalties. A large number of the choir also swopped their allegiance with him. He used to confide to people that he was very unhappy at leaving St Mary's.

Percy founded and conducted the St Cecilia Choral Society, now known as the Bach Choir, and also conducted the Ipswich Bach Choir. In addition, he also found time to lead the Stowmarket and Clare Choral Societies.

He retired from the Cathedral in 1957, where a plaque to his memory was erected in 1960.

Percy's assistant organist was Leonard Faires, ARCO, who had also been assistant to George Boutell. He was a seed merchant in the town and lived in Guildhall Street.

Clifton C. Day 1937–1942

Clifton Day, Mus.Bac., FRCO, learnt the organ with Percy Hallam and was appointed to the post of organist on his recommendation, having been organist at Diss Parish Church. His family owned Day's Footwear in Abbeygate Street, a shop which still bore the name until quite recently, when it became a mobile phone outlet. He died in 1949.

Dr Adcock 1942–1948

Dr Adcock was a doctor of philosophy, not music, and taught history at Thetford Grammar School. He covered during the difficult war years when organists were in short supply because many had been called up to help with the war effort. He lived in Northgate Street with his wife and was by all accounts a quiet and rather unassuming man. Ill-health forced his resignation.

Norman H. Jones 1948–1969

Norman Holford Jones, FRCO, LTCL, was born and bred in Ilford, Essex. He was a chorister in Ilford under Percy Saunders, later to become organist of Doncaster Parish Church and Wakefield Cathedral.

His first appointment was at St Thomas, Becontree, then All Saints, Squirrels Heath and a ten-year appointment at St John's, Seven Kings. He was appointed to St Mary's in 1948 and stated that the choir was at a low ebb. At his first choir practice he started with fifteen boys, but there were only nine left at the end. (I understand that a number were well past retirement!)

He was a teacher at Pakenham School when he first arrived in Bury St Edmunds, later moving to St Edmundsbury School, and Ixworth Modern School when it opened in 1957.

Unable to retire properly in 1969, Norman went on to be base choirmaster at USAF Mildenhall, and part of the organists' rota at All Saints Church, Bury St Edmunds. Norman Jones died in 2006.

John Fear 1969–1980

John Fear MA, FRCO (CHM), ADCM, originally came from Truro, where he assisted at the Cathedral. His early career was interrupted by war service, in which he was captured and held in a Japanese POW camp.

His music degree was from Keeble College Oxford. An extremely competent player, he held an honorary title as a 'Queen's Organist', as he used to deputize for the Chapels Royal. He was organist at All Souls Church, Langham Place for a number of years and was employed by the BBC as accompanist for the Daily Service.

He held the post of organist in at St Mary's in conjunction with the post of music master at King Edward VI Grammar School, transferring to St James' Middle School in 1972. He resigned the post of organist in June 1980 and eventually retired to Truro, where he died in 1996.

David Ivory 1980–1982

David Ivory sang in the choir and had been assistant organist to John Fear. There were over twenty enquiries about the post when advertised, and David was unanimously selected from a short list of three, taking up his appointment in November 1980.

He has been employed at Balaams Music in Risbygate Street for a number of years as an instrument repair specialist, and is curator of the Mechanical

Music Museum in Cotton, where his considerable ability as a player and as an organ restorer have been well employed.

David is highly regarded as a performer locally and nationally and has given a number of popular recitals, not only in churches but on electronic and theatre organs. His post was covered by assistant organist Trevor Hawkins until the arrival of Peter Tryon.

Peter Tryon

Peter Tryon FASC, ARCM, ALCM, AVCM, Cert. Ed., Leeds, came to St Mary's in April 1983 after being organist at Rougham Parish Church. He has been music co-ordinator at Beyton Middle School since 1978, when he first moved to Suffolk.

Born 1954 in Cambridge, but brought up in the Portsmouth area, he was a chorister at Havant Parish Church, where he first received organ lessons. In 1970, at the age of sixteen, he was awarded a county organ scholarship to study the organ at Winchester Cathedral under Alwyn Surplice and later Martin Neary. He combined this with the post of organist at All Saints Church, Winchester. In 1972 he left Winchester to train as a teacher at Bretton Hall College of Education near Wakefield. This he also combined with the post of organist at nearby Darton Parish Church.

On leaving Yorkshire he was appointed a music teacher at Gordano School, Portishead, near Bristol. He had two organist posts during this time: initially as assistant organist at All Saints, Clifton, and then as organist of Portishead Parish Church.

Apart from the organ rebuild, a number of events have occurred during his tenure of office. The choir has travelled extensively, singing at most major cathedrals, including St Paul's, York and Lincoln. Other special events have included singing for the Festival of Remembrance in the Albert Hall, recordings and singing on the back of a landrover with over 50 people and a piano for the BBC Noel Edmonds 'Late, Late, Breakfast Show'! However, the highlights must be two foreign trips to Israel and Turkey. The former included singing at over 30 sites and the first-ever choral evensong at St

George's Cathedral in Jerusalem. In Turkey the choir sang at the sites of all the seven churches recorded in the book of Revelation.
He has been most ably assisted since 1992 by

Adrian Marple, BA, ARCO, LRAM, Dip ABRSM, who is director of music at Stoke College, a regular accompanist with Suffolk Opera, a tutor on the annual summer school 'Lights, Music, Action', and a member of the jazz group Sidetrack.

Adrian began to study the organ at the age of twelve while he was a chorister at St Peter's Collegiate Church, Wolverhampton. From there, he studied at Durham University, where he was Organ Scholar and choirmaster at Hatfield College, graduating in 1984 and gaining his diploma as an Associate of the Royal College of Organists in the previous year. He then studied at the Royal Academy of Music under Alan Harverson, and was a double prizewinner for organ and piano accompaniment. After working in London as a teacher and freelance musician, he moved to Suffolk in 1992.

Memories of St Mary's Choir

The choir of St Mary's must rank amongst the longest established choirs in England, if not the world. It's unbroken history, even during Puritan times, is fairly unique. Five hundred years plus, and still going! Below are some thoughts from ex-choir members.

Leslie Bridges, Monitor Boy
written in 1992

I was about nine years old when I joined St Mary's Choir in 1924. My brother was already well established and was one of the leading boys. He was gifted musically and in later years became a very capable organist and choirmaster at Lavenham, and head of music at the old King Edward VI Grammar School. I'm afraid I wasn't very musical but was rather reluctantly made to follow my brother into the choir.

The organist and choirmaster was Mr E. Percy Hallam, who did so much for music in Bury and was greatly respected and much admired. To the choirboys, however, he was known as 'Porky' Hallam, a most unsuitable nickname as he was slender and elegant, but I imagine the 'Porky' was an understandable misreading of his dashing signature 'Percy' Hallam.

There was an entrance test conducted by Mr Hallam before the Monday night practice in the Lady Chapel. First, reading was tested with some verses from the psalms; then repeating notes played on the battered harmonium kept in the Lady Chapel. My reading was much better than my singing, so I was admitted as a 'probationer', which entitled me to wear a cassock but not a surplice. A probationer had to attend choir practices, but on Sundays had to sit on a ledge round the organ stool until some further test enabled him to wear a surplice and join the end of the two stalls of choirboys. Even though I passed, Mr H. did say he thought I needed to have my tonsils out — a craze just then. A visit with my mother to Dr Hinnel proved that this was not necessary. Incidentally, John, my brother, had had his adenoids removed by the same Dr Hinnel, who operated on a table in a bedroom in Bloomfield Street.

I think two or three other boys were admitted on the same night as I was, and we assembled in the vestry at 7 pm on that first Monday with the established boys. All wore cassocks and took their places in order, two rows of forms set along the south and west walls of the vestry. Cassocks and surplices were concealed under red curtains behind the seats. Mr Hallam wore his cassock, and at the given time the two columns of choirboys processed in silence from the vestry, through the nave, and took their places in the front choirstalls.

The probationers were at the rear, shepherded by a 'monitor' for each side. The latter were boys whose voices had broken but who willingly stayed on in the choir. He walked at the rear and 'looked after' the little boys on the second stall. I became one of these monitors and also a 'book boy'. The latter job I loved. It meant going early and putting out all the books and anthem sheets, and finding places. I also often went in on Saturday mornings to sort out music, mend it, and so on. There were large cupboards in the Suffolk Chapel, which was then not restored, and there was a door into the inside of the organ to the left of the console. In there I found piles of bygone copies of *Punch*, which made most interesting reading — cartoons about Russian bears, Disraeli, Gladstone, Bismarck — all several years old.

I can only remember one boy rejoining as a man — an alto. All four front choirstalls were filled, but for the practice some of the boys moved from their stalls to make a more compact group. There must have been about 24-30 boys in the choir then. On Sundays they had to wear Eton collars (starched ones preferably, but celluloid ones were tolerated) with black clip-on bows which had to be tucked under the collar. A mortarboard with a blue tassel would be purchased from Smart and Farries (now Bodyshop). This had to be worn on Sundays and was used to carry the books for the procession from the vestry to the chancel.

There were usually three practices a week: Mondays and Wednesdays for boys only, and Friday with the men. Practices were at 7.30 pm or so, and always lasted an hour or more. On Fridays the boys came at 7 or 7.15, the men joined at 8 pm, and the practice went on another hour or hour-and-a-half, or even longer. At the boys-only practice, Mr Hallam used the harmonium for accompaniment and 'starting off'. This ancient harmonium was trundled out from the Lady Chapel by two eager volunteers and placed in the centre under the chancel screen. Mr Hallam could play standing up and pumping with one foot, and often conducting with a series of batons which he frequently broke by tapping (if annoyed) on the edge of the harmonium's lid. This was dented and even splintered by fierce baton attacks. The great organ was not used for boys-only practices. On Fridays the assistant organist often came. He was Mr Faires, a seed merchant by profession, but a very able amateur musician. Mr Hallam took great pains over the psalms and canticles. There was always an anthem for Sunday Evensong, except in August when practices were reduced to one per week. In those days the psalms were 'as set' in the *Cathedral Psalter*, so we had to take the long and the short, morning and evening. The anthems and communion settings were typical of the time: Maunder, Parry, Wesley, Stanford, Stainer, etc.

The organ was the original Walker instrument, three-manual and hand-pumped. For services there were always two people pumping, but often one had to suffice for Friday practices, when Mr Hallam was requested not to use 'too much pedal'. During the long sermons the two pumpers would often go out of the north door and smoke their pipes in the churchyard — the strong shag tobacco smell sometimes drifting in. On one Sunday evening I remember that the sermon was abnormally short, and when Mr Hallam tried to play the post-sermon hymn there were no pumpers present. He banged furiously on the pedals, the men rushed in, and the organ wheezed into life.

St Mary's was then very Low Church. There was no cross on the altar and wafers for communion were considered 'popish'. The choir was needed for Matins, Evensong and one monthly Choral Communion which took place after Matins, so we had to be there from 10.30 until 1 pm.

Congregations were certainly large in those days, but, in the Victorian tradition, Matins and Evensong congregations were different. Traditionally Matins was for the 'gentry', professional classes and superior tradesmen. Regular worshippers were members of the Lake family (the brewers), doctors, etc. Some still wore frock coats and top hats, and there were plenty of bowlers. At Evensong, the humbler people came, such as artisans and small tradesmen. At both Matins and Evensong the nave was mostly full, with a fair sprinkling in the side aisles. No woman dared appear hatless.

At Choral Communion there would be long queues of communicants reaching from the choir right down the nave. At Harvest Festival the church was really packed to capacity and chairs were put all along the nave and aisles, and in the Lady Chapel. The choir usually had a long processional hymn and processed along the aisles and down the nave. The verse 'At last the march shall end' was sung standing still; 'Then onwards' — off with a surge.

When I joined, the vicar was Dr Herbert Branston Gray, the former headmaster of Bradfield College where, as a great classicist, he had an amphitheatre built for the performance of Greek plays. Alfred Blundell, the well-known local artist, had made an etching of the theatre — it used to hang in the old Feoffment School which I attended until the age of eleven.

Dr Gray was quite a character. For services he always wore his scarlet doctor's gown. In the procession from the vestry to the chancel he always walked a few steps, then paused, then a few more, then another pause. There were usually two curates to assist him. His sermons were long — always about 30 minutes, and he hated interruptions such as coughing. I remember once he stopped speaking and said he could not continue until coughing stopped — it was only a matter of self-control. The rest of his sermon was heard in silence. The bishop's sermons were at least 40 minutes long. That was the second bishop I saw — Dr Whittingham. The first was Dr David, who went to Liverpool. The visit of the bishop was a great event. His chaplain always came with him, carrying the long case containing the crozier. The choir had to be ready early and wait in respectful silence.

On Sundays there was Matins at 11 am, followed, once a month, by Choral Communion, Evensong at 6.30 pm and a children's afternoon service once a month or so. The organ was then played by an elderly lady called Mrs Cockburn.

The Suffolk Chapel was not used, as the organ took up half of it. So it was like this on the Sunday nearest to Armistice Day, when either the British Legion Band or the Suffolk Regimental Band played the hymns, etc, for the service. They sat in the chancel in front of the choirstalls. I remember the puddles made when they 'emptied' the brass instruments during prayers. On one occasion the trumpeters for the Last Post (six of them) stood precariously on top of the chancel screen.

I recall going to at least one Assize Service. Before the Assizes opened, the judge and other local 'big-wigs' attended a service at St Mary's, it being a civic church. The procession, led by the judge, was greeted with a fanfare of army trumpeters and everything was very impressive. The judge I remember was Lord Hewitt, the then Lord Chief Justice.

Once a month or so there was a church parade service by the members of the Suffolk Regiment in the Lady Chapel. (The Suffolk Chapel was not opened again until a rebuilt organ was installed.) Prebendary Carlisle took such a service one Sunday morning before Matins — he accompanied himself on a small concertina.

I was in the choir when Prince Henry (then recently made Duke of Gloucester) unveiled the Yeomanry Memorial in St Wolstan's Chapel. During the service he was taken for a tour of the church. I've rarely seen any visitor looking so bored!

Unfortunately, for some reason, I was never present at the annual Benefactors Service.

St Mary's Choir was sometimes asked to sing at weddings or funerals in neighbouring villages, although the only one to which I went was the funeral of the Dowager Marchioness of Bristol at Ickworth Church. Her tiara (or coronet?) was on a crimson cushion on the coffin. We were each paid 7/6d (37½p) for the attendance — a handsome sum for those days.

We were always paid for the normal choir work once a quarter (I think). Mr Samuel Smith, the then headmaster of the Boys Feoffment School, was choir fund treasurer, and we would sit on the benches in the vestry and wait for each name to be solemnly called and receive the money. I think the head boys got 10/- (50p) and others downwards to about 1/- (5p) for probationers.

The verger was a great character called Thomas Reeve. He rang the curfew every night at 8 pm — St Mary's tolls followed by a number indicating the date.

The bells were rung every Sunday evening and competed with those of St James' in the Norman Tower, causing pandemonium.

John Bridges, Head Boy
an extract from a letter written to his niece in 1992

... I am sorry to hear of the decline of St John's Choir. It was never 'great shakes' in my day. The feud between St Mary's and St James' has gone on for many years (centuries?). When I was a chorister at St Mary's, bloody punch-ups on dark practice nights were not unknown. C.J.H. Shann (Cathedral organist) complained to E.P. Hallam (St Mary's organist — later Cathedral organist). The latter (secretly delighted at a Marian victory) expressed mild horror — and told us all to be peacemakers and 'not vex Mr Shann'!

Arthur Bean, Assistant Organist

My attendance at St Mary's must have begun in the autumn of 1953 when I was required to enlist at Bury Barracks for National Service. I had developed an enthusiasm for church music, and particularly organ music, in my early teens and had taken organ lessons from the organist at Eye Parish Church. Being anxious to continue this, I took the opportunity to seek an appointment with Norman Jones, who kindly agreed to give me lessons.

It was with some awe that I found myself sitting on the organ bench, faced by four keyboards stacked before me. How could one possibly play the top keyboard without falling forward or resting elbows on the other three! Two rows of keys and a pedalboard had seemed more than enough to be going on with — but *four*!

Having thus introduced myself, it seemed sensible to attend Sunday morning service, particularly as this enabled me to get out of the barracks. As it happened, Norman Jones noticed me in the congregation and invited me, resplendent as I was in my khaki battledress, to sit by him on a chair next to the organ console, which in those days was situated behind the choirstalls. It was all most impressive. Thus began my involvement with St Mary's. Soon I was learning to play a wide variety of organ music from Bach to Rheinberger, Norman being particularly fond of the latter.

Early in my acquaintance with Norman it became clear just how much of a persuasive character he could be. I remember that during an organ lesson he quizzed me as to my singing ability and suggested that it would benefit my musical training if I sang in the choir — he was also on the lookout for an alto. I had sung treble at church and at school , but I had no experience of anything except singing 'the tune'. However, I had occasionally sung seconds and that sounded nothing like the tune!

On attending choir practice I realized that there was a vast difference between making sounds on a keyboard and using vocal chords at the level of pitch demanded of altos — added to which it was necessary to sing other than 'the tune', which at first led to my chords taking on a different sound from those intended by the composer. Fortunately there were others who had already got the pieces 'under their belts', which helped this novice find his feet. Norman was also the very best of choirtrainers and he helped me find my head voice and how to pitch intervals.

Imagine then the impression made upon me by the music at St Mary's where we sang almost everything in harmony and an anthem at every service. The boys' voices had to be heard to be believed, singing out in the superb acoustics, supported by a fine set of men and Norman's magical accompaniments. Anthems particularly special included Quilter's 'Non Nobis', MacPherson's 'Raise the Strain', 'Arise in us' by Shaw, and 'The Radiant Morn' by Woodward. However, the other lasting memory was the blue haze which used to pervade the church from the old coke stoves, and the cold in the choirstalls, where we choristers huddled together for warmth with feet and fingers like blocks of ice and visibly red noses, not to mention the vapour from our breath. Our cassocks also bore the musty odour of dampness. Norman, on the other hand, had the benefit of an electric fire under the organ stool.

Upon conclusion of National Service I returned home, albeit my family lived some twenty miles from Bury.

It did not take me long to discover that if I got up early on a Sunday, I could catch a train to Bury and get home by bus at night. On that first Sunday I arrived at St Mary's about 8am. The only person there was Mr Walters, the verger, stoking the furnaces, giving off their smoke. He, bless him, invited me to his home opposite the church — he and his wife making me welcome with tea and toast. Subsequently, when Norman got to hear of my Sunday perambulations, he and his dear wife invited me to spend Sundays with them at their home. For many years I was a guest there for lunch and tea, for which I owe them a debt of gratitude in providing what was virtually a second home. Eventually I was able to buy a moped, which overcame the travel difficulties.

There was a great deal going on in those days. I recall concerts by eminent recitalists and times when the organists of St Mary's and the Cathedral swopped consoles for special events. I also remember the special Regimental Services for the Twelfth of Foot and other regiments.

I remember well the choir suppers, which were held annually for the men of St Mary's and St Peter's. They were prepared and cooked by some of the ladies in the respective congregations. Afterwards there were speeches, and I have memories of one from a Revd F, a retired clergyman who always used to preach with his eyes shut! Was this for inspiration, or didn't he like the look of St Mary's congregation?

In those days it was often difficult to find boy choristers willing to undertake the regular attendance at church, although, once 'hooked', the majority entered into the spirit of the thing. The probationers received only a matter of old pence, but there was always the promise of weddings. In addition to choir work, Norman arranged for the boys to enjoy sport activities — cricket in summer and football in winter — all of which helped to create the feeling of 'family' together, with annual outings to Walton-on-the-Naze. There was also Christmas carolling. This was very popular with the boys, who expected to be rewarded with soft drinks, sausage rolls and mincepies.

There were, seemingly, always occasions requiring the attendance/involvement of St Mary's Choir, the chief of which was the most spectacular, the Bury Pageant to celebrate Magna Carta. We must have looked very colourful, processing down into the Abbey Gardens.

One of Norman's dearest wishes was for a choir practice room. We were, for years, sharing the vestry with the clergy. Then we discovered the crypt was unused. Thanks to the generosity of Mr Lofts in supplying the materials, the conversion was able to take place.

I got married in February 1960, with Norman on the organ. The full choir turned out to sing, for which I shall always be grateful. I had met my wife at St Mary's.

It was a sad occasion for me when Norman decided to call it a day, since he was a man held in great affection and esteem. The new organist was John Fear. Canon Godfrey described him as the finest organist St Mary's had ever had. It seems that he didn't greatly enjoy playing St Mary's organ and described the keyboards as like playing on puddings. He took the boys with him to sing at Truro Cathedral. Apparently there was some real fun and games there, with the older boys dressed up in sheets in the 'wee small hours' in an endeavour to persuade the younger boys that there was a ghost or ghosts!

St Mary's has therefore figured greatly in my life. It is with great affection that I recall many happy memories.

Trevor Hawkins
written in 2001

In 1968 John Fear became organist at St Mary's. He also held the post of music teacher at King Edward VI Grammar School, which was on the site of the present St James Middle School.

With family in Truro in the form of his mother and sister, who was the principal nursing officer for Cornwall, he very quickly arranged for St Mary's Choir to sing choral evensong in Truro Cathedral for a week during the summer of 1969 while the cathedral choir was on holiday.

Being short of altos, he invited me to join them on this trip, the only provision being that I had to join St Mary's Choir. As I had been in the boys' choir at St Margaret's in Kings Lynn before moving to Bury in 1968, and I also wanted organ lessons from John, I agreed to take up his challenge. The following paragraphs are a few of the memories that I have of this trip, and further trips which followed over the period of the early 70s.

On the first occasion we hired a Mulley's coach for the week and set off from St Mary's. 1969 was before much of the country's major road structure had been put in place, and with no A14, M11, M25, etc, the journey took 13 hours to complete on the first Saturday. Arriving in Truro, the choirboys were to stay in the old choir school behind the cathedral, and the men in the canon treasurer's house just round the corner. The facilities were basic, and sleeping bags were to be employed on camp beds - just like camping but with a solid roof over our heads. The first night in the house was disturbed by the main town clock, which was just across the road and had a dodgy clapper. All night it chimed every 15 minutes in the form 'Ding, Dong, Ding, Clunk'!

With practices at 8.30 am every morning and choral evensong late afternoon, every day, apart from one, our time for leisure was restricted to the rest of the morning, early afternoon and, of course, the evening. On a nice summer's day our favourite haunt was probably the beach at Perranporth. We could rely on the fact that we would all be on the beach and in the water in suitable beach attire when John Fear would arrive, walking down the beach in shoes, trousers, shirt, tie, jacket and gaberdine mac — his favourite, and indeed, probably only, attire.

John was, however, a brilliant organist, and his presence at the organ of Truro Cathedral playing the entire Bach D Minor Toccata and Fugue from memory, note perfect, was both a wonderful sound and a sight to behold.

Other trips included the statutory annual trip to Lands End for the photograph under the signpost, and trips to Newquay, which has two beaches. One of the beaches is called the town beach, and I remember that one day we were swimming in the sea and all the people on the beach were waving to us. We waved back and continued swimming. It transpired that they were telling us to come out of the water as a sewage pipe had burst on the hillside and was pouring into the sea. Oh dear, this did cause us some consternation, but luckily nobody suffered any effects from this episode.

The usual pranks ensued at times, with the men finding white sheets to cover themselves at midnight, and pretending to be ghosts over at the choir school to cause minor disruption to the leaders staying with the boys. Somehow they never quite believed that we were real ghosts.

After a couple of annual visits to the old choir school, the choir were able to stay on at least two occasions at the new choir school, which was probably somewhere in the region of one mile from the cathedral. On this first time in new surroundings, John Fear stayed in his caravan, which was parked on the grass in front of the school. This was probably not a good idea, as it was overlooked by the choirboys' dormitory. Each day a packed lunch was prepared for us to take on our day trip between practice and evensong. The lunches normally consisted of some type of sandwich such as Spam or tomato. Unfortunately these were not the boys' favourites, and on one occasion the remaining sandwiches had been stored away by them and during the course of the night had been lobbed at John's caravan. First thing in the morning the men discovered that a white caravan was spattered with tomato and Spam. In order to save John throwing a wobbly at the boys, and confining all to barracks, we very quickly cleaned the caravan before he awoke.

Other pranks by the boys included setting off the fire alarm and flooding the bathroom and shower area — although the latter may have been accidental.

Throughout all of these trips the choir performed to perfection, once robed and in singing mode, with a different repertoire for choral evensong each day, which was appreciated by congregations that included many tourists during these weeks of August.

I think that our stays in Truro may have been brought to an eventual end by the cricket pitch roller at the choir school. On a return one evening by the men from the local hostelry, the younger men decided that it would be a good idea to give the cricket pitch a roll with the large roller sitting beside the field. After all, this would save the groundsmen a job during the school holidays. Unfortunately, they had not noticed that the cricket field was not level and was on a slight incline. Getting the roller started was not a problem, but rolling down the hill towards the pitch, it gathered momentum and became uncontrollable. The men let go, and now the only thing that could stop it was the cricket hut that lay at the bottom of the hill. The hut did the job and stopped the roller, but only after it had passed through one of the wooden walls! Surprisingly, this was the last year that we were invited to sing choral evensong in Truro Cathedral, or even allowed back into Cornwall!

Matthew Sunley, Head Chorister
written in 2001

Being a chorister in St Mary's Choir [1987-1993] was quite a commitment, but it was well worth it. First, and most obvious, there was the singing. I especially enjoyed working towards our big performances, whether it be practising carols for the big services at Christmas, or preparing Handel's *Messiah* or Stainer's *Crucifixion* in time for Easter. No matter what adversities we suffered in practice, we always knew we had pulled it off when we saw the faces of the congregation and the choirmaster at the end.

Secondly, we were able to sing in some tremendous places. There were many cathedral visits where we sang at one-off services. I can't easily forget the splendour of Ely or Lincoln cathedral, and a visit to any cathedral nowadays always brings a smile to my face and a mind full of memories. And, of course, St Mary's Church, our usual 'haunt', which we probably sometimes took for granted, provided fantastic acoustics for our best efforts and sent our descants reverberating around the roof.

Lastly, and not at all least, I value the friendships I made during my time in the choir. Even though it seems many years since I walked up and down the nave to sing at services, I can still return and chat with current and former choir members as if I had only left for a few days.

Tim Scott, Head Chorister
written in 2001

1990 saw the start of my singing exploits with St Mary's Choir. At the age of nine I had moved up from primary school to St James Middle School and, as it was the in-thing to do, I had joined the folk group run by Mr Ricky Wilkinson. I was not aware at the time of Mr Wilkinson's connection with St Mary's and remember being surprised when he asked me if I sang anywhere. When I replied no he asked if I would be interested in having an audition with St Mary's Choir. I went along to the church on a Friday evening and was introduced to Mr Peter Tryon, the choirmaster. I was extremely nervous when asked to sing along with his beautiful piano playing, and was very surprised when after just a few minutes I was accepted. I did not realize at this point how large a part St Mary's Choir was to play in my teenage years.

Practices were held on Wednesday evenings (just for boys) and Friday evenings (along with the men). Initially I thought that the choir was going to be more of a chore than fun because it meant that I had to give up time not only on these evenings, but also much of Sundays. However, after I had attended a few times I began to learn the routines, make new friends and gradually improve my singing voice.

Once I had passed my probationary period, I was entitled to wear a surplice over my cassock, which meant that I could look like everybody else, and my aim was to start working towards the medals which marked your progress through the choir. The colours of the ribbons showed the stage you had reached. The first was light blue, then dark blue and finally red. The tests involved your knowledge of music and Bible study and some of these could be passed with Mr Tryon on a Wednesday just before the practice started. It was a crowd of eager small choristers around the piano trying to get as many signatures as possible from Mr Tryon on their achievement cards; it was brilliant fun! I earned my first two ribbons in a good time, but the red wasn't so easy. One of the tests was to sing a solo and, although I had greatly improved my singing skills, this was a big challenge. The solo I was given was a very short but beautiful anthem called 'Lead me Lord' by Wesley. I sang it successfully and this gave me my red ribbon and the confidence to sing more solos.

I had now reached the highest level I could within St Mary's and the one thing left I wanted to achieve was the 'Bishop's Chorister Award'. This involved learning music to a much higher level and also producing a written project. I spent many weeks preparing, and the examination day which was held at St Edmundsbury Cathedral finally came. The pass mark was 100 and the maximum marks available 150. There were seven choristers from St Mary's Choir, which was one of the largest numbers our church had ever entered at one time. I did my very best throughout the day and went away feeling hopeful; that evening I received the call from Mr Tryon to say I had passed with a score of 128. All seven of us had passed and our picture was in the newspaper!

Time passed and life in the choir fell into a pattern. As well as our usual services, we sung at weddings, which gave us extra pay on top of the 'wages' we received for practices and services. Our pay was handed out three times a year, at Christmas, Easter and at the end of the summer term. Some of the money was kept back and a back-pay cheque would be given to choristers who remained until their voices broke. There were also many civic services which were held regularly during the church year. The Battle of Britain and Remembrance Day services are ones that stay in my memory because of the many dignitaries who attended and also the members of the armed forces who marched to the church and handed in the standards as part of the worship. From our places in the choir stalls we were able to see everything that went on and, being so young, felt very important to be part of it all.

Easter and Christmas were very busy times. We had extra practices to attend because of the amount of music we had to learn. Of course, the men had sung most of the pieces before, but as the boys were always changing, with new ones joining and older ones moving on because of their voices breaking, Mr Tryon had his work cut out to produce a consistently good sound with the available choristers. His standards were very high, and sometimes when we would play around too much, as we often did, he would lose his temper and shout at us.

The highlight of the boys' year would come during the first week of the summer holidays when the annual choir camp would be held. Run by the men of the choir, assisted by older boys and parents, we would spend the week under canvas, relaxing and having fun. Sites would vary and included Santon Downham and Thorpe Wood near Thetford, although in the past some of the places had been much further afield. There were traditions such as tent-hopping after bedtime and jumping the queue at the tuck shop, but we were kept in line by tent inspections each day, leading to the award of a cup at the end of the week to the best kept tent. I was tent leader three times in a row and my group received the cup on all three occasions. I was very proud of this.

After several years things began to change. Canon John Hayden was appointed as vicar, and he had new ideas for St Mary's. Our vestry in the church tower had always been old and damp, leaving our robes feeling cold and smelling fusty as we put them on. Now the inside of St Mary's Tower was being refurbished, with new rooms being constructed on four levels. The third floor became the new choir school, and although quite small, it meant that we were warm and our cassocks and surplices were no longer damp. Canon Hayden had another particular interest - travel - and it was not long before discussions began about the possibility of St Mary's Choir making a pilgrimage to the Holy Land to sing at many of the historical sites. As the possibility turned into reality we began fund-raising to reduce the amount each boy would have to pay to take part in the trip. Parents worked hard to make the idea possible, and we boys also played our parts. We advertised that we were able to attend other churches to sing at weddings, and we held a sponsored sing-in at St Mary's in order to raise money. I had moved up the ranks by this time, through Team Leader and up to Deputy Head Chorister. Imagine my surprise when the voice of the then Head Chorister, Stephen Baker, broke and I was asked to take over for the trip to Israel. I couldn't believe it!

The visit was all we had hoped for. An experience which will stay with me for the rest of my life. It was a very busy schedule, and we seemed to be always getting on a coach, getting off a coach, putting our vestments on, taking them off, singing first in one church and then perhaps singing in the open air in the hot sunshine. We swam in the Sea of Galilee, in the Dead Sea, and walked beside young soldiers carrying guns in Jerusalem. Visitors gathered to listen to our singing wherever we went and, in spite of having a cough, I sang a solo verse of 'Jesus Christ the Apple Tree' at the Mount of the Beatitudes. I was just 14 years old and the whole thing was great! Two years later another tour was arranged to Turkey to sing at the seven churches visited by St Paul. This was also a great success.

I was quite tall and it was very surprising how long my voice lasted out. When I was no longer able to reach the high notes, I moved into what was known as the back row, into the alto section. After this it was a very short time before my voice dropped much deeper and I became a bass, missing the tenor section altogether. In 1999, at the age of 18, I left to pursue other interests, but I shall never forget the experience of being a member of the historical choir of St Mary's Church. My thanks go to Mr Ricky Wilkinson for introducing me in the first place, and to Mr Peter Tryon for all he taught me over those formative years in St Mary's Choir. Long may it continue.

Nico Rice
written in 2007

I met Mr T for the first time when he came over to tune the family piano, and although I was only seven years old, he figured I could sing. I don't know how, but he did. I then turned up for the Wednesday rehearsal (just for the boys) and was broken in within a month, donning my surplice for the first time after this probationary period. Somewhere, my parents have kept the pictures of this event, and I look back at my time in the choir with great fondness — whether it was the sitting in the stalls killing the opposite rows in more and more elaborate ways (from a handgun to the always victorious mimed bazooka), or the club on a Friday night, I enjoyed the choir enormously.

My experiences in the choir stick with me — driving back from Ipswich or eating my supper on my way to choir on a Friday night from boarding school, I managed to make it to choir rehearsals thanks to lifts from Mr T himself (I apologize for dropping any breadcrumbs in your car, I know they took ages to clean out). The trips varied from lying in the boot due to the overload of passengers, to sitting in the front, and the conversations were always great — even if they did sometimes feed the gullible me with interesting stories (King Arthur was killed by a heart attack from looking at a Solar Eclipse?). I can also look back at earning my medals one by one. There were definitely large flaws in my singing, and the medals process, along with Mr T's expertise, managed to iron them out (especially my breathing). I took those things very seriously, managing to achieve the first light-blue-ribboned-medal to the final red one, with a green medal on the side for good behaviour. I can also vividly remember the test for the Bishop's Chorister award — the singing, aural and project, all of which I still keep locked away. I did work hard for the medal, and receiving it was a great source of pride for me. I even had a photo at the back of the Bury Free Press (in the TV Guide section).

These memories pale in comparison with the tours to Cyprus and Malta, in both of which I enjoyed myself immensely. It was thanks to the choir that I went to countries I would probably never have visited otherwise. Although I don't have many photos of either tour, I can visualize many events of the trips; whether it was performing in a chapel at the bottom of a block of flats, or standing on a stage in front of a large audience within a historic abbey. I was allowed to sing a solo in Malta, which I managed to scrape through, and thanks to a DVD produced by Mr Harman, I squirm watching it as many times as I like — although he did cut out my rather shaky beginning (to say the least). Singing at the various major cathedrals in the country and abroad remain clearly in my mind — from the first one I ever did, Peterborough, to the last one, St Paul's. The two which strike me are the evensongs at Canterbury and St Paul's — I had always seen them as the main two cathedrals in the UK, and so to sing in them was wonderful. I have to admit that I don't normally go out of my way to visit churches, and the choir again gave me an outstanding opportunity not just to experience them, but to perform in places of massive historical and cultural importance.

In all, I spent six years at St Mary's — joining as a shy seven-year-old, who could barely hold his breath for longer than two bars. I'm happy to say that the choir added an extra dimension to my maturing, as well as increasing my lung capacity. By the time I left, I had been Deputy Head

Chorister for over a year, and had eventually succeeded in becoming Head Chorister (though it did break the record as being the shortest reign ever, lasting about three weeks). The one thing I never managed to do was to go to the annual Choir Camp, which I heard was very, very good.

I see my time in the choir as the 'glory days' — since leaving, my singing voice has dropped around two octaves, so where I used to pride myself on the overpowering high notes, I now console myself as a low bass, content to sit in the relative shadows of the back row. During my stay in the choir, I really feel that I grew up and matured in a way that would never have been possible otherwise — it has allowed me to stand up in public without breaking down into a nervous wreck, because an element of that shyness I had when I was younger still remains with me today. When I listen to recordings of the choir from my time there, I beam with pride and happy memories. The choir was and is enormously successful, and I'm glad I was there to be a part of it. I want to thank Mr Tryon not just for bringing me into the choir in the first place, but also for driving me into town three/four times a week as I became a permanent feature in his car. He saw me grow up, both personality-wise and physically, and has become a strong family friend. Thank you.

Tom Rees
written in 2007

My name is Tom Rees, and I have been actively involved with St Mary's Church Choir for quite a long time. It has become an integral part of my everyday existence, and I believe that without my six years' singing with the choir, I wouldn't be the kind of person I am today. When I was around nine years old, I was recruited by my then music teacher, Peter Tryon, who was and is the choir master at St Mary's. He told me about the many different aspects of becoming a member of the choir, and how it can greatly benefit and improve almost all areas of life.

After joining, he was almost instantly proven correct. I met lots of nice new people whom I probably wouldn't have met under other circumstances, which was a social boon for me at the time. In addition to helping me make more friends, it was a great platform for trying out lots of interesting new things, as well as the singing. These included the impressive tours abroad, going to Malta, Gibraltar and Spain; the choir camping trips, which have become a well-loved tradition amongst both boys and men; performing in cathedrals all over the United Kingdom, including St Paul's; and many other fascinating events and excursions. During my time with the choir, I have slowly but surely risen through the ranks of the choir hierarchy, going from probationer to light blue, working my way through the medals, becoming a Team Leader, earning the Bishop's Chorister Award, becoming Deputy Head Boy, then taking the place of Head Chorister, and finally losing the voice of a young boy and becoming a young man.

With music such as Handel's *Messiah* and 'Zadok the Priest' in my repertoire, I have had to learn to be a fairly robust and self-assured performer; and having to be that has given me a fresh self-confidence in myself and my abilities, which has allowed me to become much more opinionated and outspoken in all parts of my life, making it possible for me to become the person I wanted to be.

Members of the Choir and Clergy, Summer 2007

A list of choir members on 1 January 2008

Boys

1. James Myers (Head Chorister)
2. Derek Rutter (Deputy Head Chorister)
3. Richard Preston (Team Leader)
4. Ryan Noonan (Team Leader)
5. Robbie Noonan
6. Douglas Sands
7. Jack Golding
8. William Woods
9. Matthew Last
10. Craig Gradidge
11. Toby French
12. Edward Marriott
13. James Smailes
14. Glen Dempsey
15. Cameron Brown
16. Henry Byrom-Smith
17. Barnaby Byrom-Smith
18. Peter Rogers
19. John Rogers

* Ex-boy choristers who now sing in the men's section

Altos

1. Chris Ballam
2. Tristan King
3. Tom Rees*
4. Sam O'Doherty*

Tenors

1. Alan Day (joined 1950)*
2. Fraser Simpson*
3. Daniel Harris*
4. Martyn Hawkins*
5. Alex Wilkinson
6. Hugh Brookfield
7. Maylott Robinson*

Basses

1. Trevor Hawkins
2. Ricky Wilkinson
3. John Chandler
4. Ian Goodchild*
5. Steven Goodchild*
6. Tim Hollins*
7. Barry Thomas
8. Aidan Valentine*
9. Gordon Sefton
10. Fred Walker

Choir Tours Overseas

1995 Israel
1997 Turkey (the Seven Churches)
2001 Cyprus
2003 Malta
2005 Southern Spain and Gibraltar
2007 Barcelona

Publications from Honey Hill Publishing
an enterprise of St Mary's Church, Bury St Edmunds

An Abbeygate Street Story	£2.00
The Organs and Organists of St Mary's Church	£4.00
Of Bells and Clocks and clock connections at St Mary's church	£1.50
Cyprus: a handbook for Christian visitors	£4.50
St Paul to St Nicholas: a handbook for Christian visitors to Turkey	£4.50
St Mary's Church Guide	£1.50
St Mary's Church: a photographic library on CD-ROM	£10.00

All publications can be obtained from
St Mary's Church, Honey Hill, Bury St Edmunds, Suffolk IP33 1RT.

If ordering by post, please make cheques payable to
St Mary's Church, Bury St Edmunds,
and add 60p per copy for p&p.